ANSWERS *that* AWAKEN

Answers that Awaken

Unleash the Power of Attunement in Your Life
By **Sirshree** Tejparkhi

Copyright © Tejgyan Global Foundation
All Rights Reserved 2016

Tejgyan Global Foundation is a charitable organization
with its headquarters in Pune, India.

ISBN : 978-81-8415-627-0

Published by WOW Publishings Pvt. Ltd., India
First Edition published in March 2016
First reprint published in December 2024

Printed and bound by Trinity Academy, Pune, INDIA

Copyright and publishing rights are vested exclusively with WOW Publishings Pvt. Ltd. This book is sold subject to the condition that it shall not by way of trade or otherwise, be lent, resold, hired out, or otherwise circulated without the publisher's prior written consent in any form of binding or cover other than that in which it is published and without a similar condition including this condition being imposed on the subsequent purchaser and without limiting the rights under copyright reserved above, no part of this publication may be reproduced, stored in or introduced into a retrieval system, or transmitted, in any form, or by any means, electronic, mechanical, photocopying, recording or otherwise, without the prior written permission of both the copyright owner and the above-mentioned publisher of this book. Any person who does any unauthorized act in relation to this publication may be liable to criminal prosecution and civil claims for damages.

Although the author and publisher have made every effort to ensure accuracy of content in this book, they hereby disclaim any liability to any party for any loss, damage, or disruption caused by errors or omissions, resulting from negligence, accident, or any other cause. Readers are advised to take full responsibility to exercise discretion in understanding and applying the content of this book.

Contents

Introduction

Part I Essential Spirituality   9

Part II Existential Dilemmas   16

Part III Demystifying Divinity   23

Part IV The Ultimate Goal   28

Part V Paths to Liberation   40

Appendix

Introduction

This book is a selected compilation of questions posed to Sirshree by seekers. The questions in this book range from existential dilemmas to essential spirituality. Every answer is intended to make you find yourself, know yourself, and ultimately be yourself. The answers in this book will lead you to pure consciousness, to inner stillness.

The primary aim of human life is to stabilize in the experience of pure consciousness and express its divine qualities. Only those answers which serve this purpose are of any value, whether you have heard or read them many times before.

Though you may seemingly know the answer to a question in this book, continue to read the answer, because the purpose of the book is not merely to impart intellectual knowledge, but to help you access pure consciousness.

The following four steps tell you how to read this book:

Step 1: Feel the space created by the question

Read the question carefully. The moment you do that, the question will create a space within you for the answer.

Step 2: Fill the space with the answer

Fill that space with the right answer, else the purpose of the question will be lost and mere words will remain. As you read, some insights will emerge. Some answers might transport you to a state of deep stillness. It is in this state that the answers intuitively begin to be revealed.

Step 3: Let the magic of awakening unfold

Search for yourself in the answers and learn about your true nature through them. Answers that have been understood will then manifest as actions in your life. Allow the answers to unfold in your life. Some answers are such that we need to wait before we can understand them. This is because it is essential to experience certain things before we are able to understand them.

Step 4: Park aside what you do not understand

If there are answers or concepts that you do not understand, park them aside for a while and move on to a different question. After reading the entire book, revisit those questions. They may then make more sense to you.

Answers to all questions are available at the very place from where questions originate. When this secret unfolds, you will be able to get to the core, to the source of your being. Then you will tell yourself: "No question has remained. I can now get all the answers from within myself."

PART I
ESSENTIAL SPIRITUALITY

1. **We all are born, grow up, fulfill our responsibilities, have families and then pass away... What is the purpose of all this? What is the purpose of human life?**

Sirshree: The purpose of life is life itself.

This may not seem easy to understand. When people are not ready to receive higher answers, they are told, "The goal of life is to become a doctor, or an engineer, or to be successful. If you want to become a carpenter, then become a good carpenter. If you wish to become a doctor, become a good doctor and try to gather knowledge."

Initially, such answers seem adequate. However, it is only when one is prepared to receive higher understanding that they get higher answers: The goal of human life is that life should know life. Life, in this context, refers to the inner experience of aliveness within each one of us, which is known as Self, Consciousness, *Allah*, God, Christ, *Ishwar*, Lord, and so on. It is the living (sentient) consciousness due to which this body is alive and moving. In the absence of the enlivening consciousness, the body would be a mere corpse. The body, by itself, is insentient. It comes alive only because of the Self, the living entity within us. Let life return unto itself; let life experience its own essence. When the life principle in a body is consciously aware of itself, it is called Self-realization. 'The goal of life is life itself' means that the purpose of human life is to attain Self-realization and to be stabilized in that experience.

The underlying meaning behind this answer is that you should know your self (your true self, your original nature). It is only in order to know your true self, and express the life within you, that you have been associated with your body.

When you know the real meaning of life, you will also understand the art of 'being life'. We feel that we should be taught the art of living. But you don't have to learn the art of living; you need to become life itself. Your personality is not leading life. Life is enacting your personality. You have to rise beyond the body.

Up until now, you have lived by assuming yourself to be a body. You identified yourself with your body and would have often said, "This person told me this, he appreciated me, they made fun of me..." However, all this happened not with you, but with your body (the body–mind mechanism).

Let us try to understand the meaning of 'life returning unto life' further. When you raise your level of consciousness to its pinnacle, only oneness remains. You experience the inherent oneness of all beings and objects in the universe. The goal of life is to attain the experience of that oneness and be established in it.

To understand this in even simpler words, it can be said that the goal of human life is to open up, blossom, and play the game of life. This implies that you have to explore all the possibilities that lie within you. The complete possibility of an individual is realized only once he opens up fully, blossoms fully, and plays out the entire game of life. This means that once he realizes that it is God's game that is being played out on Earth, he too will begin to play this game in the right manner, and only then will he achieve the purpose of life. God, refers to Consciousness, the Source of everything, the very essence of life itself.

Every being on this Earth starts out on this path; just as every flower in the garden sets out to bloom. Before blooming fully, some flowers break from the stem, some are blown away by the wind, some are plucked, and some are eaten by worms or destroyed by disease. But the purpose of each flower is to blossom fully, and to spread its fragrance to one and all.

We should see what system or path we can follow to reach our goal as fast as possible. This is the goal for every human being. However, when we are not aware that this is the purpose of our life, we don't work at it. Only when it becomes clear do we start working on it. Then we won't miss a single opportunity that helps us to progress on the path of truth.

2. **What is spirituality? What is its relevance in practical living? Is it required in our daily life?**

Sirshree: Understanding our true nature through direct experience is spirituality. It is a common notion amongst many that spirituality is not really essential to practical living. Let us understand why spirituality is essential with the help of a short story.

There was a strange tribe that lived in a jungle; strange, because they chose to be always blindfolded. They plucked roots and fruits, reared live stock and made handicrafts. However, they performed all these tasks, blindfolded. Hence, they kept stumbling, falling, and colliding. It was difficult for them, yet this was the way they had always lived.

One day, one of these people went to another village where his blindfold was removed. He was able to see and was amazed. He returned to his community and told everybody that they too should go to the place where blindfolds are removed. He said they should get the strips pulled off their eyes because it would be extremely beneficial for them all.

One of those people replied:"I don't feel there is any real necessity to do this. I just don't have the time." What would you say? Surely, you would say, "If you remove your blindfold, you can do everything faster and better."

All those people who are leading their lives blindfolded by false beliefs do not feel the need for spirituality. When we are surrounded by such people, even we may not feel the need for it. But if we want to come out of the darkness of ignorance, then spirituality is essential for us.

People question the need for spirituality only because they do not know what it really is. When you understand the real meaning of spirituality, this question will not arise. If you are among those who consider that applying vermillion on the forehead, wearing saffron clothes, garlands, and rosaries is spirituality, then this is an illusion. True spirituality is about knowing your own essence, recognizing who you truly are.

Is it necessary to perform all the rites and rituals: rise early in the morning, read the scriptures and perform worship, dip a lotus in water and sprinkle it on everyone? Well, such activities are not spirituality; they are merely reminders of spirituality. People mistake these reminders (the medium or method) as spirituality. This makes them question the necessity for spirituality. When reminders of spirituality are viewed as spirituality itself, or when the means become the end, things can go quite wrong. The medium or method is not the goal: it exists for achieving the goal.

3. **Can we experience the blankness of deep sleep when we are awake? Even after a lot of effort, I am unable to attain that experience. The mind keeps pulling my attention. Why does this happen? Why am I not able to experience the state of inner stillness?**

Sirshree: Samadhi is the state of timeless existence that you can consciously experience in the waking state. With practice, you can wakefully experience the state of no-mind, just as you experience blankness during deep sleep. Actually, there is no need to explicitly bring that deep-sleep experience into the waking state, because it is already present right now. The reason you are not able to experience that state is because you have your own concepts and imaginations about it. You keep comparing what you experience with your imaginations.

The mind compares both experiences–waking and deep-sleep. In deep sleep, the feeling of the body disappears; pain and suffering are absent. The mind expects to wakefully experience this state. When effort is made to wakefully experience it, the mind may complain: "My head is throbbing and my back is aching. Why can't I experience the blankness devoid of body sensations when I'm awake?" Until that experience is truly recognized, it seems very subtle and difficult to grasp.

Let us understand this further through an example. You are sitting in a room where soft music is being played. You are asked to listen to the music. But there is a lot of noise and commotion in the room, due to which you are unable to hear the soft music. You would say, "Stop this noise; it's preventing me from hearing the music." But even when everything is silenced, you are still not able to hear the music because you have preconceived notions about the music too. You are trying to listen for music that is familiar, which you have heard before. If the music that is in your memory is not being played, then you won't recognize or properly hear the music that is being played. Gradually, once you begin to understand the new sounds, you realize: "This is music too! I was comparing it only with my preconceived ideas." Now you begin to perceive it. Then you experiment to see whether you are able to hear the music even when there is noise all around. When you get attuned to that music, you will be able to hear it even in the din and roar of the surroundings.

In exactly the same manner, when you are able to experience consciousness in a peaceful environment, you will gradually begin to experience it in commotion too. Then you will realize that this is what you also experience during deep sleep. You realize that this experience of consciousness has always been present, it never left you.

So what remains to be done now? Well, nothing. Just sit or lie down and keep watching the scenes that appear before you. When a scene appears, watch it. When it does not, then experience the presence of consciousness in which scenes appear and dissolve. This is very simple. But at first, when you try to grasp it, your imagination draws a picture of the experience of consciousness. You compare it with the blank state of deep sleep.

Your mind also places stipulations on the experience by saying, "It will feel this particular way in this part of the body with this intensity." This is the method of seeing with the mind. But the mind needs to be told that such stipulations are unnecessry. The imaginary ideas of the mind are great obstacles. No sooner does the mind hear about anything, it immediately assumes and fixes imaginary pictures about it.

The sense of conscious presence is constant. When you sense your presence, you realize that your living presence is the same as it has been since childhood. No change has taken place in your presence. A lot of things have changed externally, but internally your living presence is constant. There is a feeling of continuity through all these years because your presence has not changed within you. Your sense of aliveness is still the same as it was during childhood.

Try to remember what you looked like in your childhood. Many people simply cannot believe that they looked as they see themselves in their childhood photographs. Yet you still do not feel that you have changed because there is one thing in common between your past and present states, due to which you proclaim," I am the same 'I', which was present during childhood." What is it that is still the same? It is easy to grasp, as it constantly exists. Your height, weight, everything else has changed. Nothing is the same, except your sense of presence. It is this presence that you experience in deep sleep, and which you want to feel in the waking state. Just get rid of your imaginary ideas about it.

4. Is the experience of Consciousness or Presence within us or outside us?

Sirshree: When it is said that the experience of consciousness is constantly going on within each of us, you might imagine that it exists within the human body. However, consciousness is not just within the body. Rather, the body exists within consciousness. All of this existence is happening within consciousness.

Think of a fish living in water. Water is an all-pervading presence for the fish. It is the essential medium that keeps the fish alive. Water exists not only within the fish, but also all around it. Water is so close to its eyes that the fish doesn't realize that it's in water. What if the fish swam off in search of water, asking, "Where is water?"

This is precisely what the questioning mind would ask when it is told about the all-pervading nature of consciousness: "Where is this consciousness? Is it within me, or elsewhere?"

The experience of presence or consciousness is your very essence; it is who you truly are. You will find that the spatial concepts of *within* and *outside* are relative to your body and belong in the realm of thoughts. From the standpoint of consciousness beyond thoughts and words, there is neither within nor outside. You are consciousness.

It can be said that Consciousness is outside both inside and outside. This may sound illogical but understand this with an example. Suppose there is a person hiding in a closet. There is another person in the room outside the closet. A third person is watching these two from the opening through the roof of the house. The person who is hiding in the closet is *inside*. The one who is in the room is *outside*. But the third person, who is watching these two, is outside of *inside* as well as *outside*. Consciousness is local and non-local. It is all-pervading and transcends the concepts of space and time.

Part II
Existential Dilemmas

5. Conventional texts state that desires are a cause of sorrow. Is this true? Is it fine for me to entertain worldly desires?

Sirshree: Desires, by themselves, are not the cause of misery. It is attachment to desire that leads to endless seeking, craving and frustration. Attachment implies a sense of obsession, infatuation or fixation. To be free from attachment is to be free from suffering.

Attachment to relationships, roles that we play at home or the workplace, titles, money, comforts and conveniences, lead to the habit of acquisition and preservation. Being identified with idea of an individual 'I', we seek gratification in the external world. We are constantly engaged in acquiring what we lack and preserving what we fear we may lose. This tendency of acquisition and preservation entangles us in the vicious cycle of attachment that leads to sorrow.

Attachment or obsession occurs when you live as a claimant, claiming ownership of objects, relationships, homes, etc. When you lay aside your claims, knowing that these objects and relationships are impermanent and have no bearing whatsoever on your state of happiness, you will no longer be attached to external objects or people. Does this mean that you lose your love and passion for life and its affairs? Not at all! The passion will still be there, and yet, it will be a detached passion.

You may desire worldly comforts and pursue them, until you find that they do not give lasting happiness. You then seek what can give you true fulfillment. You go after spiritual pursuits. The habit of desiring is still going on. Earlier you desired material objects; now you chase spiritual imaginations.

You cannot be free by letting go of your attachment to any particular object or person, because it is then replaced by something or someone that you consider to be 'better'. In other words, you cannot give up anything, unless you hold onto something that seems 'better'. And then you get attached to the 'better' thing.

You can attain true freedom from all sorrow only when you let go of *the one who is attached* – the limited separate individual who you assume yourself to be. When you cling to your limited identity of being a unique individual, separate from totality, you are bound to experience fear, sorrow and anger. From attachment springs the fear that your desire may not be fulfilled, sorrow when the desire does not bear fruit, and anger with whoever or whatever seems to obstruct it.

The solution lies in steering clear from thoughts that are based on the limited 'I', 'me', and 'mine'. Insulate yourself from the grip of the idea of the limited personality that you assume yourself to be. You need to first rise above this 'I', 'me', 'mine' and see them for what they truly are. Then you can engage in the world without being attached.

6. **Is it essential that we do something for others to give them peace and comfort, even if it causes us inconvenience? Is the maxim –** *In the wellbeing of others alone lies our happiness* **– a valid belief?**

Sirshree: 'In the wellbeing of others alone lies our happiness'—this is true. However, there is one word in this maxim which should be questioned, and that word is 'others'. Who do we consider as 'others'?

It is important to break this false belief that there are 'others' who are separate from 'I'. The vast population lives in the illusion that whatever is inside the body-skin is 'I' and whatever is outside is 'others'. This illusion is so deep-rooted in the human psyche that the inherent oneness of who-we-truly-are is completely missed. Since we see everyone else believing this illusion, we never question it.

There are no 'others'. In essence, we are all one. The universal 'I' is functioning through each one of us. The entire world is an integral whole; there is no separate individual, no second person. One sun gives life to the entire world; the same air breathes life into all bodies; one nature sustains life everywhere. The all-pervading consciousness alone is. Separateness is illusion.

When you rise above individual necessities, you begin to be sensitive to the necessities of 'others'. When your life is no longer personal (self-centered), you begin caring for the wellbeing of everyone. You go beyond the individual 'I' when you become one with your family. When your span of identification extends beyond the family, it becomes one with the neighbourhood. It can expand still further to encompass the group or community, and further to your country, and even beyond to identify with humanity. Thus, you rise beyond the individual 'I' and identify with the collective 'we'.

However, when the false 'I' dissolves, the Self alone exists. There is neither an individual 'I' nor a collective 'we'. The Self expresses itself through totality. If 'X' helps his neighbour 'Y', it is like one finger of the hand helping its neighbouring finger. Upon Self-realization, it is the hand that is helping itself through the interplay of all the fingers.

When you begin to experience the joy of leading such an impersonal selfless life, both 'I' and 'others' are non-existent. Service becomes a natural and spontaneous expression of who-you-truly-are. The inconveniences that occur in rendering service fade into insignificance before the sheer bliss of Self-expression.

To answer your question, when the Self is realized, then it is no longer essential to do something for others by sacrificing peace and comforts. This is because Self-service is all that remains. There is no question of sacrificing anything, since Self-service is service from the Self unto the Self, arising out of the bliss of experiencing the Self.

7. **Man comes into this world alone and leaves this world alone. Why then does he marry? Why does he beget children? What is the purpose of these relations?**

Sirshree: It is indeed essential to foster associations with relatives to live in this world. The deeper purpose of relationships is to enable you to mature and learn vital lessons such as uncompromising love, compassion, unshakeable peace, unconditional joy, tenacity, patience, perseverance, and being in harmony with life itself. For this, you need a mirror that enables you to see all facets of your mind. Without the world-mirror, you will not be able to witness your own mind.

The world is not as it appears to you; the world is how your thoughts are. Your world is a screen upon which you project your own mental patterns, your unresolved emotions, your strengths and deficiencies. What you view as the world is, in reality, a reflection of what you project.

We constantly shape our own personalized worlds as we go through life. People, situations, the weather–everything we experience–are shaded by our perceptions and are projections of what is held deep within our minds. We mould the personalities of people around us through our own beliefs and assumptions. This occurs without our awareness, and we may probably find ourselves criticizing people for shortcomings, without realizing that these shortcomings could merely be projections of our own beliefs. We experience our own unresolved emotions by unknowingly projecting them on people. For example, when someone seems to be angry or deceitful to you, he or she is actually reflecting the anger or deceit, which is unresolved within you.

This may seem a bit farfetched to believe in the beginning, but when you experiment with this truth, you will see how the world has been infallibly mirroring your beliefs. Though it may seem unbelievable, you're actually attracting situations and people into your daily life according to the emotions, traits, and beliefs you harbour within your mind. You tend to be invariably lost in external details to such an extent that you don't realize that these details are only living pictures of what lies buried within your mind. External situations are not the cause, but rather a reflection of what you hold within.

It immensely helps to be constantly aware that the people around you and the situations in your life resonate with the thoughts you entertain. Every trial, every situation, every person you meet in life, has been consciously or unconsciously chosen by you, so as to enable you to imbibe divine qualities and mature.

It is possible to unravel our limiting beliefs only amidst relations. When a relative tells you something, you may perhaps get irritated. If they tell you something else, you may probably feel pleased. You can witness such vagaries of the mind only amidst relationships. What are the underlying fears or beliefs that make you behave the way you do with them? Our relatives serve as mirrors to reveal ourselves, to uncover the fears that lurk within us.

The eye needs a mirror to see itself. Similarly, a person needs a mirror in the form of relationships and incidents to recognize the faults within. Discover how and in which relationships you have been creating suffering for yourself and others. Use every complaint to look within and achieve clarity. Instead of working on changing others, work on clearing your own limiting beliefs.

Once you focus inward and work on your shortcomings, the world will not appear the same. Gradually, you will begin to realize that this world is a marvelous system that resonates with your nature. Your kith and kin serve as a mirror in your life to enable you to see your true nature.

Witness every member of your family, every friend, every colleague, as a co-creator in your life. They are present in your life to help you grow, to realize your highest potential. They are here to help you develop an unshaken, pure and unconditionally loving mind. Such a mind alone can serve to experience the grandeur of the Self and express its divine qualities.

8. **I want to make progress in today's competitive world, to earn a name, fame and wealth. I want to accomplish a lot in my field of activity. Is it spiritually wrong to pursue and acquire money?**

Sirshree: Many people often have such questions: Is it wrong to acquire fame or wealth? They wonder whether material success can ever go hand-in-hand with spiritual growth.

They seek to enjoy a perfect life, with harmony in relationships, financial freedom and physical vitality. They wish to hone their creative potential and achieve worldly success. But they feel constrained by limitations and fall victim to the uncertainty of life. They lose inner peace in this pursuit of material success. There are others who seek inner peace and a deeper meaning to life. However, inner peace and lasting fulfillment seems to elude them as they are drawn into the demands of daily living. Hence they feel that spiritual progress cannot accompany material growth.

There is nothing inherently wrong with money or any other object of pursuit. It is the urge of pursuit itself that is wrong. Everything in the world has been created for you in abundance; you need not pursue anything. You only need to be receptive in order to receive these things. Just be present; always be centered in the experience of Self-awareness wherever you are—at home, at the workplace, in the market— in whatever you do. Perform your role sincerely, and all those things that are required for your divine purpose will naturally come to you. You need not struggle to achieve anything. Your very state of calm receptivity attracts everything that you truly need in your life.

You should assess your actual needs. If you mistake a rope in the dark to be a snake, you might search for a stick to beat the 'snake'. Here, the need felt for a stick is not wrong. But ask yourself, "Is the stick really needed?" Since the snake is merely an illusion, the stick is not really needed. If you are making effort to acquire something that deviates from your actual needs, then it does not lead to fulfillment. What you actually need is a torch that can help see the rope as a rope. Then the need for the stick will vanish.

In the same way, when the ultimate truth about life is comprehended in the light of understanding, your needs may naturally undergo a change. You may find that what was a necessity earlier in the absence of wisdom, can be dispensed with.

The utilization of money, skills and qualities undergoes a change when you keep the spiritual purpose in mind. Things, which were earlier utilized for indulging in the illusions of the world, will be utilized for realizing the true purpose of life. Thus, while you continue to engage in the material world and earn wealth and fame, how you relate to them can change completely.

While you attain wealth and fame, it is also important to acquire some vital qualities like patience, resilience, consistency, equanimity, creativity and courage. These qualities are the key to realizing your highest potential. Develop these qualities through the various situations that arise in your life.

When you put to use the pearls of wisdom in the right way, you will find that money comes to you naturally. You will then utilize money appropriately. When people lack the higher understanding of life, they keep accumulating money and magnifying its value, without putting it to the highest use. This is like a person who keeps polishing his shoes throughout his life, but never sets out on his journey. Money is only a means; not an end. Keep the end in mind while earning money. You can then attain both–inner peace and worldly success.

Part III
Demystifying Divinity

9. Does God exist? If God exists, then why can't we see Him? How can I develop faith in His existence?

Sirshree: Some people question why God can't be seen; they doubt whether He exists in this world. We live in a world where "seeing is believing." Hence, whatever is unseen or intangible is considered to be non-existent. Breeze is unseen, but the grass in the fields sways, announcing the presence of breeze. You conclude by inference that breeze exists, though you don't see it.

Suppose a child sees someone, completely veiled in a long cloak, walking down the street. He says, "See that empty cloak is walking." You will explain to the child that an empty cloak cannot walk by itself. There has to be someone inside the cloak. The child may contend, "But I can't see anyone there." You would then explain, "Just because you are not able to see anyone there doesn't mean that there's no one."

The human body is like the cloak. God is the enlivening consciousness due to which the body comes alive. It is due to the enlivening consciousness that the body can walk, talk, know and act. Asking whether God exists is like asking whether there's butter in milk. Since butter is not visible in milk, would you say that butter does not exist? No. There is a process of churning through which butter can be extracted from milk. In the same way, to experience God, you need to seek the essence of life within you.

Expecting to see God with your eyes is like trying to hear music with your eyes. Listening to music has nothing to do with eyes. You can never grasp anything that is not visual with your eyes. If you are expecting to see God, you need to understand that He is everywhere. Consciousness pervades the universe. It is the knowing principle that enables you to see. You cannot refute God's existence, because God is the essence of 'existence' itself!

Suppose someone is lying down with eyes closed and you ask him, "Are you sleeping?" If he says, "No, I am not," you will conclude that he is awake. But what if he replied, "Yes, I am asleep." Even if he says he is asleep, it only means that he is awake. Else, how would he be responding to you? In the same way, when one says that God exists, it means that God exists. Even if one says that God does not exist, this too means that God exists. What is enabling him to speak and say that God does not exist? It is the same knowing principle, the underlying consciousness that enables him to say so. God is that consciousness.

People who watch mythological TV serials or movies are used to imagining God in the image of Lord Rama, Lord Krishna, Jesus or Buddha. Moreover, they hold the images of actors who enact these roles and expect that God could appear only this way. If that is the way you want to behold God, then you cannot. The mind wants to see God, but it should attain the understanding that God cannot be seen in terms of a fixed physical form. When the mind is infused with this understanding and develops faith in the existential nature of God, it surrenders its insistence to experience God or consciousness based on its own imaginations.

10. **Why did God create this world? Is it because He was not happy without creating it? If God is perfection, then what was the need to create a world that is imperfect?**

Sirshree: When a nightingale sings, would you ask why it 'needs' to sing? No. Singing is not the nightingale's need; it is its nature. It's only man who assesses everything in terms of needs and benefits. Just as a bird sings, the world too is the song of God! There is no need of the word 'need'.

Have you ever known a painter who has never created a painting!? No. A painter creates paintings to express himself; painting is a means for him to realize his creative potential. In the same way, the world is a painting by God. The sole purpose of the world is for God to realize Himself through His creative expression.

Just as a painter expresses his unexpressed potential through his art out of sheer joy, the world too is an expression of bliss from the pure unexpressed state of God. God exists in the state of causeless bliss. When happiness is at such heights, then creation of the world is bound to happen.

Many people wonder why this world has been created. They question the very purpose of existence. Those who are depressed complain about life. They see this world as an imperfect place. They blame an imaginary creator for creating an imperfect world. People often wonder: Why are some people deceitful, while others are noble? Why do some people sing melodiously, while others sing harshly? Why do some people appear beautiful or pleasant, while others appear ugly? Some go even further to the extent of concluding that it would have been better if this world were never created.

The fallacy in their thinking is not very obvious. The missing link in their understanding is a very subtle one. If the creator had never created this phenomenal world, replete with its beautiful variety, if those people who complain about imperfections were never created, how would it ever be known whether creating the world was good or bad, whether it was useful or useless? Something has to exist first in order to know how it is. If nothing existed, there would be no question of knowing!

A painter mixes the fundamental colours (red, green, blue) to create new derived colours. He uses many colours including black. One may wonder why the painter has made 'black', as it is appears dark and depressing. However, for the painter, black is as important as any other colour. Thanks to black, he is able to lend depth to his art. In some cases, black actually highlights and enhances the beauty of other colours by offering a contrast.

Some people sing harshly, but they are also important in the Creator's plan. If it were not for them, then those who sing melodiously wouldn't be valued. Similarly, deceit fulfills its higher purpose of elevating the value of goodness. Everything that exists has its importance. The world, in its entirety, is perfect in all its apparent imperfections. But if we look at everything from our limited perception, we will develop preferences and get into the habit of comparison and judgment.

We need to think from the creator's point of view. What is the creative intention? Why create things that we label as 'bad'? The ultimate purpose is benevolent. The sole intention of creation is to experience and express the highest creative potential. Where there are mountains, there are bound to be deep valleys. Without the white background that pervades paper, you cannot recognize the writing in black.

We need to understand the cosmic game being enacted in the world. We need to understand our role in the scheme of things. When we lack the higher perspective of life, we see imperfections.

11. **How does one recognize God? Can he appear in any form – as a child, a downtrodden or a saint? Is this why we should live with love and compassion for everyone?**

Sirshree: If you are looking for a fixed method of recognizing God, then you can never identify God through any external method. The mind wants to verify and confirm that God will come adorned in ornaments or in a particular costume. This is a myth. After seeing movies, mythological TV serials, and poster images of God, we attempt to recognize God in terms of what we already know through these media.

Once you experience God as the living consciousness within yourself, it will be easy to recognize Him outside your body too. You will recognize God's presence as the all-pervading consciousness in all forms, both living and non-living. Myths and stories create a misconception that God incarnated only in certain bodies. But everyone and everything in the universe is His form alone. When you experience your living essence—the conscious presence—within yourself, you will realize the same presence in every body.

Our living existence that we are intuitively aware of, is exactly the same within every body. It is this very experience of aliveness, which is the Source of everything. It is this Source that has been called 'God', 'Self', 'Lord', 'Allah', 'Higher Self', and so on. Be it the body of a child or of an adult, of man or woman, of a rich man or a poor man, this inner experience is the same.

We can recognize this divine presence within others only after having experienced it within ourselves first. This experience can be known only by being that, not by *thinking about* that.

Part IV
The Ultimate Goal

12. What is Self-realization? Is it truly the ultimate goal of life? Isn't there anything beyond?

Sirshree: Self-realization is the realization of our oneness with Consciousness through experience of our true nature. We live by assuming ourselves to be our body and mind. When we experience our true nature as pure consciousness, beyond the body and mind, it is called Self-realization.

We live with the belief, "I am the body". When we clearly know the fallacy of this belief, the underlying oneness of everything is experientially revealed. The limited individual personality, that appears due to identification with the body, dissolves. The universal 'I', the real 'I' is realized.

Self-realization is the state of liberation from ego, from mechanical living, from fear, worry, anger, from bondage. It is freedom from our preconceived notions. It is the experience of unbroken bliss, which is indescribable, without a cause, which constantly asserts its eternal presence and pervades every aspect of life.

Whatever we pursue in our worldly life is only the foreground. Self-realization is the background of all pursuits. It is the aim behind all aims of life, because it is the art of 'being' life itself. It is the fulfillment of the very purpose of human life.

Is there anything beyond Self-realization? It can be said that Self-realization is just the beginning. Self-stabilization is the goal.

There are many who experience momentary flashes of oneness when they are with nature or even in the midst of their daily lives. However, these are only samples of the experience of Self-realization, mere glimpses that happen when the understanding of our true nature shines forth.

Such glimpses of Self-realization are experienced when the interfering and comparing mind momentarily becomes silent. But what happens after the glimpse? The mind emerges again and takes credit for the experience: "I performed meditation; I attained this deeply profound state; I experienced Self-realization." The mind lacks the understanding that it did not experience that state. On the contrary, when the mind was stilled, the Self experienced itself. Self-stabilization is when the comparing and interfering aspect of the mind does not emerge. It is not just a one-time experience. It is about permanently and constantly abiding in the experience of pure consciousness. One lives with the firm conviction of one's true nature beyond the body and mind. Self-realization without understanding is futile. It is meaningless to proclaim that you have attained Self-realization based on a one-time experience, without being stabilized in the state.

Self-stabilization is the ultimate purpose of life. If the body continues to indulge in old tendencies and habitual patterns even after many such glimpses of the Self, then the ultimate purpose is not served. The judgmental mind keeps returning with false beliefs and doubts about the experience of the Self. Due to this interference of the judging mind, the state of inner stillness in which the Self experiences itself remains veiled.

The importance of a true Guru is that he ensures that you progress from Self Realization to Self stabilization. A true Guru teaches you to train the mind by instilling it with the understanding of truth so that the Self can experience itself without interference.

With Self-stabilization comes Self-expression – the expression of the Self through the body-mind mechanism. On attaining Self-stabilization at the age of thirty-five, the Buddha continued to spread the message of Truth till the ripe age of eighty. Siddhartha Gautama's body served as a medium for expression of the Buddha (Self).

When the purpose of Self-stabilization is not clear, you might mistake glimpses on the path as Self-realization and assume that to be the ultimate goal. If Self-realization is seen as Self stabilization, then that is the ultimate goal. If you see it as a one-time experience, then it is just the beginning.

13. What exactly happens with Self-realization?

Sirshree: On Self-realization, you return to the original state of pure unexpressed consciosuness. The one who forgets the original nature of the Self gets entangled in the vagaries of the mind. But the day he remembers the immaculate state of the Self, he also remembers the purpose of life in this world. He realizes the temporary nature of the world.

The original state of the Self is at rest when the world is not created – an unexpressed state where the Self alone exists, where the knower alone exists without anything to be known. This is the state when the experiencer is present, but cannot experience himself.

When there is only one without another, one cannot know oneself. It is only when there is 'another' that one can feel one's own presence. So as to experience the Self's own presence, the Self-in-Rest brings about the state of Self-in-Action… the expression of the Self. The subject creates the object, so as to experience its own presence. When the Self manifests as the mind comprising thoughts, it is the state of Self-in-Action. The Self experiences itself through expression.

However, when the Self gets identified with the mind and body, it assumes "I am the mind, I am these thoughts, I am this body." This gives rise to an illusion of many separate bodies, many separate selves, due to the notion of separateness. So, if I am 'this' body, it assumes that I am not 'that' body, or 'those' bodies. So whatever is inside the body-skin is assumed to be 'I' and whatever is outside appears to be 'others'. However, this is merely a projection, an illusion that the Self gets entangled in. In this entanglement and false identification, the real purpose of this expression—the purpose of experiencing itself—is forgotten.

When Self begins to dis-entangle from this illusion of separateness, inner Self-witnessing gains precedence over witnessing the world. The ultimate purpose is realized only when there is a permanent shift from 'witnessing the world' to 'witnessing the witnessor'. While looking at a mirror, if you do not see yourself, then the purpose of the mirror is not served. In the same way, while witnessing the world, the focus should shift to witnessing the Self (knowing the knower). The world serves as a mirror to bring awareness of the presence of the knower.

When Self-realization is attained, the conviction about falsehood of the separate notional individual is established. The original nature of the Self is recognized. The Self continues to be in action, and yet remains dis-identified from the mind-body.

The Self's false identification with an assumed individual separate personality, comes to an end. The individual may feel that he is attaining Self-realization. But, when Self-realization actually happens, the imgained idea of being a separate individual disappears. Thereafter, everything happening through the body is impersonal Self-expression.

14. After Self-realization, what changes take place in our lives?

Sirshree: After Self-realization, what happens is not change, but transformation. Change is just an alteration; transformation is a paradigm shift. For example, when you begin to climb the stairs to reach the terrace, you move from the first step to the second. Though this is a change, you are still on the stairs. When you move from the second step to the third, you can probably get a better view of the terrace, but you continue to be on the stairs. This is 'change'. When you move beyond the stairs onto the terrace, this is called a shift or 'transformation'.

With change, ignorance continues, because you still perceive from the level of the mind through judgments, logical premise, assumptions and memory. However, with transformation, the entire structure of the programmed mind is transcended. You rise above mental perceptions (the stairs) and intuitively know from the Source (the terrace).

Suppose you are sitting in a room where there are pillars that block your view of the entire room. You keep changing your position in the room, so as to get a better view. However, you still cannot see the room in its entirety as the pillars obstruct a complete one-time view. But when you get into a helicopter that hovers above the room, you get a complete simultaneous view of everything as it is. You are also able to see what the others in the room are not able to see and which pillars are blocking their view.

In the same way, before Self-realization, you keep refining your perspective by going around beliefs (pillars) that block the experience of reality. You keep changing your perspective. However, rising beyond all beliefs, the mind (the room) is transcended and a holistic all-encompassing view of the reality is intuitively known by the Self. This is transformation.

Life then becomes an expression of the qualities of consciousness (God). None of this arises out of any careful thinking or deliberate force. It happens naturally, with ease, because it is your original nature. You do not need to think about your true nature; you just need to be who-you-truly-are. However, thoughts are essential for whatever is not your true nature. When questions like "How should I do this?" arise, the question of 'how' only arises in matters that are not your true nature. For example: How should I live? How should

I deal with this situation? How should I make this decision? How can I get rid of sorrow...? As long as you get such thoughts, you are away from your true nature. When you abide in your nature, all such questions end. You will not need to know 'how to'. Every answer, every solution shall reach you on its own.

After Self-realization, one transcends the opposites of happiness and sorrow, attachment and aversion, praise and censure, life and death. For example, it is a common belief that the Self-realized one becomes mild or humble. 'Becoming humble' presupposes the existence of a separate individual who has 'become' humble. However, Self-realization is the transcendence from both –ego and humility. There is liberation, not only from sorrow, but also from happiness. It is liberation from duality. The separate individual who says 'I have attained Self-realization' no longer exists.

15. **I was in the feeling of divine grace for some days after attending a spiritual retreat. I was in the experience of the Self. But my mind is again becoming restless and disturbed. How can I be free from this restlessness?**

Sirshree: In the journey of stabilizing in the experience of Self, it is important to understand the role of the judgmental mind, about how it keeps coming back amidst glimpses of Self-experience. During this journey, even if the judgmental mind keeps coming back a thousand times, let it happen. Treat it like the coming and going of clouds that temporarily veil the ever-present sun.

Like the eternal sunlight, Self-experience is constant. It neither comes nor goes; it neither increases nor decreases. Your awareness of Self-experience may reduce or can rise. When you have no worries—when nothing in the external world has occurred to increase your thoughts and there are no concerns about the future— the experience of the Self seems more prominent. But when difficult situations arise, it seems as if the experience of the Self is lost.

This can be understood, with the example of a TV that is switched on. The TV screen is lit up. However, in the afternoon, if the windows of the room are open to sunlight, then the TV screen will appear faint. Due to the brightness of sunlight in the room, you may not be able to clearly make out that the TV screen is lit-up. When windows are closed and curtains are drawn, then it may appear as if the TV screen has become brighter. But, you know that the TV screen is the same. It has neither dimmed, nor become brighter. It is just that you have become more aware that the screen is always lit.

The mind can become frustrated and disappointed when it feels disconnected from the experience of Self. This happens due to the lack of understanding that these very feelings of frustration and disappointment are the cause and not the result of disconnectedness.

The analytical mind tends to make a tangible goal out of everything that is pursued. However, accessing and abiding in the Self is not a tangible goal. It is the enlivening presence in which all pursuits of life are undertaken. Hence, positing a goal and defining expectations cannot lead to the experience of the Self.

Since every external pursuit in life is quantified or qualified in material or tangible terms, the mind tries to set expectations for the purpose of experiencing the Self as well. It will desire to experience such objectives as peace of mind, tranquility, deeper intuition, or greater creativity. If it doesn't immediately see such results, it feels disappointed. It then gives up by assuming that the pursuit is impossible or futile.

The key is to see through all such expectations as the play of the judging mind. Being the Self is the way and the end in itself. You are already at the destination during the journey. You just need to be present, and let feelings of disappointment or frustration arise and pass by.

Allow the mind to rise; let go of the feelings of frustration and disappointment. You don't need to be worried every time it bounces back. Every time you watch the mind rising and falling, you develop conviction in your state of inner stillness that is constantly available behind the mind. With increasing conviction, the mind will gradually become still.

16. Do thoughts stop appearing when we experience the Self?

Sirshree: Being in the experience of the Self does not mean that there won't be thoughts. Thoughts of the intuitive mind may continue to occur and enact through your body. To be in the experience of Self, thoughts of the contrast mind need to be transcended.

All of us have an aspect of mind that can be called the Contrast mind. During infancy, every child abides in the experience of the Self. However, as the child grows, the parental programming and social conditioning lead to the formation of this contrast mind.

The contrast mind is that facet of the mind that discriminates, compares and judges everything. It is the constant chatter that ceaselessly comments about everything that is experienced. Just like the contrast control on a TV remote control, which is denoted by a circle with black and white halves, the contrast mind too dwells in duality. It divides everything into silos and labels objects, beings, or circumstances as good or bad, happy or sad, black or white, dark or light, positive or negative, low or high, benefit or loss, and so on.

The contrast mind draws assumptions and judgments. Whenever you notice yourself thinking: "This shouldn't have happened… That should have happened… Why does it always have to be me? Life is so difficult… When will these people change", this contrasting facet of the mind is at work.

The thoughts of the contrast mind are based on the root belief, "I am the individual; I am the body." Thoughts of the contrast mind cease when one dwells in pure consciousness, in the experience of the Self. The individual "I", the imagined idea of "I" dissolves. Pure consciousness remains alone, conscious of itself. However, thoughts of the intuitive mind may continue to occur and serve the expression of the Self.

The intuitive mind functions spontaneously, based on natural intuition and inspiration. Unlike the contrast mind, the intuitive mind is focused on the present task and performs it to the best of its ability. It is free from comparison, judgment, labelling and fixation. Thoughts of the intuitive mind are harmless and constructive.

Thoughts that arise from Self-experience transcend the desires or ambitions of the individual 'I'. Such thinking naturally arises from a deeper understanding where one does not feel separate from the rest of creation. Instead one identifies with everything and everyone as One. Life is led in service of others with the conviction that all are One. When one is established in this conviction, then every event is seen from a universal perspective rather than an individual biased viewpoint. Thoughts that lead to Self-expression continue to occur.

17. Is a Guru required in the spiritual journey? What is the role of a Guru? How do I recognize a true Guru?

Sirshree: The word Guru is made up of two syllables 'Gu' and 'Ru,' meaning darkness and light. Guru means "One who dispels darkness." Darkness refers to ignorance, delusion, false notions and beliefs.

Is a Guru required? The answer to this is simple: Is a mother required? The answer to both the questions is the same. There are some children who don't have mothers and yet they grow and thrive. Similarly, there are a few who didn't have a Guru and yet have attained enlightenment like Guru Nanak, Ramana Maharshi or Gautam Buddha. In most cases, a Guru is required, as in the case of Saint Tukaram, Saint Gyaneshwar, or Saint Kabir. Some external body acted as their guru. It is in rare cases that enlightenment is attained without a Guru. This is because the Truth can be revealed only when the mind surrenders completely. The mind, by itself, cannot make the mind surrender. Another body on whom you have faith is essential.

There are some who argue that a Guru is not needed and then there are some who spend all their time arguing that their Guru, their religion, and their portrayals of God are the correct ones. Because they are focused on the wrong thing, they never attain the Truth. To understand whether a Guru is required or not, it's first important to know who the Guru is.

Do you consider a person as the Guru? Is it the body? No. Many people are caught up in this confusion. They have been told, 'this particular person,' or 'this body' is your Guru. You aren't supposed to approach anyone else or attend any other teachings. If you do so, you're disloyal. People lead their lives with this fear of being rejected.

A body is not the Guru. The Consciousness, which manifests through that body is the Guru. The Consciousness within you that is yet to be revealed is the Guru. It is that Consciousness that guides you. It may guide you through a person, a book, or dream. So what do you have to do? Just be open and receptive. Don't close yourself saying that if others can attain Self-realization on their own, then I can too. That's not in your hands. Just be open and let Consciousness guide you.

A living Guru is important because he can guide you according to the nature of your body-mind mechanism. Therefore, you progress fast. When he sees you, he understands how far you've come and what your hurdles are. The teachings and the instructions delivered by the living Guru have a very deep impact. If you try to hit someone with a bullet held in your hand, the bullet won't have an impact. But the Guru is like a gun. When the bullet of wisdom is shot from the Guru, it hits the person with tremendous momentum and causes a deep transformation in his life. If the disciple listens to the Truth from someone who is not a true Guru, then the impact is like the bullet thrown from the hand. When the disciple listens to the same words, the same knowledge, from the true living Guru, his ego is eliminated.

How do you identify your Guru? Your Guru is where your mind calms down and where its habit of vacillating in thoughts subsides. Your Guru is where you become free of deceit. If the mind's habit of vacillating in thoughts begins to diminish, you are at the right place. The true Guru will lead you towards the state that transcends thoughts. The true Guru dissolves your beliefs, your false notions. In fact, it is in the Guru's presence that the disciple starts transcending the mind and body. Once you are in contact with your Guru, your life is transformed.

The right Guru has the complete understanding of Self Experience, the state of liberation, the state of Oneness, the timeless state of Beingness (Samadhi). The true Guru is Self-realized and is able to guide you towards Self-realization. The One who has attained liberation alone can lead you to the Truth.

Attaining human life is the first grace. If the thirst to attain the ultimate truth of life arises within you, then that is the second grace. When the disciple is ready, the Guru has to appear. The appearance of the Guru in your life is the third grace. If you are able to develop unshakeable faith in the Guru, then this is the fourth grace. It is with God's grace that you receive a Guru. And it is with the grace of the Guru that you realize God. This is the ultimate grace.

18. **I have understood that being stabilized in the state of Self-realization is the goal of life. But how do I attain it? How do I begin? Which path of seeking is suitable for me?**

Sirshree: There are many paths that lead to stabilization in Self-experience. But they can be fundamentally divided into just two. The Path of wisdom is the path of will power, where effort needs to be put in. It is like a baby monkey that needs to hold onto its mother's belly when it jumps from one branch to the other. The other is the Path of submission, where there is no need for any effort as there is complete surrender. It is like a kitten, which leaves its body loose and gives itself up to its mother, who then carries it around with her mouth.

There were two travellers who needed to cross safely through a jungle to return home. One of them was blind, while the other did not have legs. Individually, they could not have made it home. The lame traveller climbed onto the shoulders of his blind companion and started guiding him through the jungle. The blind man followed his directions and walked carefully, carrying him through the jungle. Both managed to reach home safely.

So it is on the path of Self-realization. The lame man symbolizes the eye of wisdom; the blind one represents the legs of devotion. Without the legs of devotion, the eyes of wisdom cannot walk the path. And the legs of devotion cannot see the path without the eyes of wisdom. Let devotion obtain the eyes of wisdom and let wisdom in turn receive the legs of devotion.

All the paths that are known in spirituality finally culminate in this two-fold path—one approach is that of complete surrender, while the other is that of intellectual reasoning and meditation. The seeker of Self-realization needs guidance on both these paths. The Guru delivers wisdom through the medium of meditation and Self-introspection. The Guru kindles faith in the heart of the one who follows the path of wisdom, which leads the contrast mind to surrender completely. The Guru delivers wisdom to the one who follows the path of surrender. Finally the one who works on gaining wisdom surrenders and the one who surrenders attains wisdom. Thus, both the paths merge at its culmination in Self-stabilization.

However, you do not have to decide which path is best for you. Whatever the mind prefers need not be the best path for you. Following the path that the mind feels like is like asking a thief how he would like to be captured. The contrast mind has to drop. Leave how this happens to grace. Ultimately, grace is the only way!

Part V

Paths to Liberation

19. **During the Magic of Awakening retreat, we were taught to practice shifting our attention to the heart, which I did. But I could not see any divine light then; there was only darkness. Later, while contemplating upon your teachings with eyes closed, I could see a beautiful divine aura, which led me into stillness. I felt immense joy. What was that state? Was it the experience of the Self?**

Sirshree: While placing your attention on the heart, you couldn't see any 'divine' light, which then appeared later during your contemplation. It is very important to understand this: In which light did you see that light? You need light to see anything. However, there is also the invisible light in which you can see light itself! This invisible light is that of awareness, the inner knowing. It is beyond the realm of sights, sounds and feelings.

You mentioned that when your attention was directed inward, you saw no light but only darkness within. In which light did you see that darkness? It is the light of knowing, the light of awareness in which you perceive darkness. When that light is witnessed, awareness becomes aware of itself. The light of consciousness, which shines upon everything that is being known, becomes self-illumined. The Self experiences its own presence.

When people do not recognize this light of knowing which is constantly illumining their life, they mistake the light they envision during meditation to be the goal. Seeing any visual light or hearing divine music are mere milestones on the path. They are indications to move ahead. You do not stop at milestones by assuming that you have arrived. Similarly, on seeing some form of light, you don't have to stop there. You do not have to get stuck at these experiences of light or sound because the true experience of the Self lies in experiencing consciousness, which enables the seeing of light or darkness.

Many, who practice meditation, get attached to mystical visions. They treat such visions as a sign of having arrived at the culmination of the journey. They miss the light of awareness in which these visions are being witnessed. Self-knowing does not seem attractive as there is nothing in it for the mind. The experience of nothingness does not seem like a worthy result to the ambitious mind. Seeing divine light seems more appealing. It is very important to understand this.

The other important aspect is the judging and comparing mind that comes into play. You experienced joy by witnessing the light. But the contrast mind now compares that experience from memory with what is being experienced today. It seeks an identical experience, and hence it is not open to what is available right now. The experience of the Self is available here and now. But the insistence of the contrast mind to experience the Self in terms of past experiences becomes a major hurdle in the journey. Due to this folly of the mind, it becomes difficult to be stabilized in the experience of pure consciousness.

The experience of the inner light, in which everything is being known, is fresh, lively and spontaneous. It need not be compared with the past. It has always been and will always be. All other experiences at the physical plane of the body will come and go. We do not have to get caught up in these physical experiences.

20. What is prayer? What is meditation? Which of the two is more important?

Sirshree: Prayer is the means to manifest life. Prayer is not merely what is ritualistically practiced with folded hands and closed eyes. Every thought that receives your attention is a prayer. Prayer is put up to the Source, or the Universe, or the Creative principle. Everything is available to be experienced in life. Prayer leads you to a state of receptivity so that what you are praying for can manifest in your life.

In the context of manifesting a good life, if prayer is the question, then meditation is the answer. Prayer is only half the secret of creating what you aspire. Meditation completes the secret. Meditation is the full secret. People focus on prayer, on creative visualization and manifestation techniques based on the law of attraction. But they miss the all-important need to meditate. You ask for something through prayer. But then you have to be in silence to receive the answer. In other words, being in meditation makes you receptive and attuned to the creative principle, so as to receive what you have prayed for. This is a missing link.

Prayer is also offered before meditation as it helps us to enter the receptive state of meditation. But the greatest prayer commences when we are fully immersed in the state of inner stillness during meditation. Abiding in that state of silent receptivity is the ultimate prayer beyond words. When a body enters that state, it becomes fully receptive to the Source of everything. The mere presence of such pure being is the greatest prayer for the universe.

Thus, being in the state of meditation is the ultimate prayer. When you consider this perspective, prayer and meditation are both the same. From the other perspective, you begin with prayer and culminate in meditation. You ask through prayer and receive through meditation. The answer depends on how we look at it.

21. How do I witness my thoughts so as to detach from them?

Sirshree: Thoughts should be witnessed for what they truly are. To understand how thoughts are witnessed, take the example of your favorite song or music that you love. Take a pause and try to remember the song or music. Remember the details of the tune, the accompaniments and the lyrics. Hear it in your mind. Now, how did you hear the music? You cannot answer this in words. The song just played within your mind. Your external ears didn't hear it, and yet, you were aware of it! Isn't this amazing!?

In exactly the same way, when thoughts arise, you are aware of them. You need not explicitly think about the thoughts. You are implicitly aware of their rising. Thoughts are known in the light of awareness, which is your true nature. Everything manifests from consciousness, exists in consciousness, and dissolves into consciousness. With alertness, you can use thoughts as reminders to focus on the presence of consciousness instead of focusing on the content of your thoughts. Understand how thoughts can be witnessed so as to detach from them.

During festivals, we see fireworks that light up the night sky. Flares rise up in the sky, create a dazzling display of forms and colours, light up the sky, and then die down into the emptiness of the sky. The flares can take any shape. It can be a display of a happy smiling face, or even a sad frowning face. You enjoy seeing the fireworks regardless of the form that the flares show in the sky.

Thoughts can be witnessed as flares that arise in the sky of silence. Regardless of the content of your thoughts, you can enjoy the wondrous display that arises in the vast stillness of consciousness. Who-you-truly-are is permanent, eternal. Thoughts come and go. They are like flares that shoot into the night sky. They appear for some time and then fade away in the sky of eternal consciousness.

When we see a firework expressing a frowning form in the sky, we do not feel depressed. Instead, we marvel at it and exclaim: "What a fantastic invention! How did the firecracker do that?" Similarly, worrying thoughts may arise in the space of your awareness and say: "What will happen to me?" "How can I manage this situation?" Regardless of what the thought says, you can merely witness it and marvel at the miracle of how thoughts arise within your awareness and then dissolve.

However, when you get stuck with your thoughts, you identify yourself with them and assume, "This is happening with me." Then you feel depressed. But you do have an alternative. You can derive joy from every thought, positive or negative, merely by witnessing them like fireworks in the sky of awareness. When you watch a thought merely as a thought, without focusing on the inherent meaning of its content, you will be able to enjoy the fun! You will learn the art of watching thoughts by being detached.

Thoughts also serve as a double-headed arrow. While thoughts carry worldly content and meaning, they also convey the fundamental news that you are alive, that consciousness is present in the background of thought. Thoughts – whether they are trivial and mundane, or brilliant and revolutionary – serve as a medium to indicate the presence of the Self. You can become aware of awareness itself through the pretext of thoughts that arise.

We always focus on the meaning of the content that our thoughts convey. Suppose a thought occurs: "It's such a lovely and sunny day!" This is the content of the thought, but it is primarily conveying your essential presence, that you are alive and aware. We are so obsessed with the content of our thoughts that we miss this fundamental truth.

As a daily practice, you can raise your awareness of awareness itself, by remembering the presence of consciousness within which thoughts arise. For this, you need not ignore the happenings of the world. Of course, you will heed them and take necessary action. However, everything that happens is an opportunity, an invitation, to shift to the underlying truth that all this is coming alive in the presence of the Self.

The Self is ever-present as the witnessing awareness in the background of thoughts. Even during deep sleep, when there are no thoughts, the conscious awareness is continuously awake and knowing the sleep state. When there is nothing to be known, even the nothingness is being known. It is only due to the presence of awareness that you know that you slept well after you wake up. The body and mind disappear during deep sleep. You are neither the body nor the mind, but the knower of these. The more you are convinced of this, the more you will be detached from your thoughts and established in pure consciousness.

22. **What is true action? Isn't every human action actually a reaction to situations? Is it possible to have pure action, which is not reactive?**

Sirshree: Reaction is a programmed response that depends on external or even internal stimuli. The subconscious mind has been designed to automate responses to certain stimuli. Since childhood, we observe and learn certain fixed responses. The subconscious mind is the storehouse of such fixed responses. For example, we don't need conscious interpretation to pull our hand away from fire. The subconscious mind is programmed to automatically enact this response to the stimulus of fire. They are the learned behavior that you borrow through your genes, upbringing from parents, neighbours, at school and through the media.

Reactions can be simple, like your responses to everyday physical situations, such as suddenly braking the car to a halt when an obstacle appears on the road, or gripping onto something when you stumble. Reactions can also be behavioural responses to complex situations, like your response when you feel cornered in a group discussion or your withdrawal from a social scene where you sense insecurity or discomfort.

When someone swears at you, you may be programmed to swear at him as a reaction. If someone praises you, and you feel gratified and comply with their needs, it is a reaction. This means that your swearing or complying with people is dependent on their actions. It means that you have handed over the control of your life to people and situations. Most people lead life in a reactive way, being a victim to their programming.

Reactive living does not need higher awareness. You do not need awareness to follow the same beaten path every day. However, if you have to choose a new path, which is unknown, you need awareness. Creative living requires higher awareness. Human evolution is all about moving from reactive living to creative living; it is about raising the level of consciousness.

When the wisdom of karma awakens, your responses will be increasingly intuitive and creative. Your actions will arise from conscious choice based on higher understanding. For example, if someone swears at you, you will choose an awakened response by either ignoring it or responding creatively. An awakened response is not constrained by fixed behavioural patterns..

When one says,"The situation was such, that's why I got angry" then it is a reaction, even if it is dependent on circumstances. We react either impulsively or compulsively to others' actions. For example, when one says, "I will study if my friend also studies; I will exercise every morning if you join me; I will practice meditation only in the group", then he is following a reactive way of living. His actions are not based on any careful independent consideration or understanding of his own. He is dependent on his friends. When he moves from living reactively to an awakened life, his understanding will be: "I will study, exercise, and practice meditation every day, even if others don't, because they are good for my mental, physical and spiritual health."

An awakened response is an inspired action that arises from intuitive thought. It does not arise from the storehouse of programmed responses. It is fresh and creative, arising from pure consciousness. Actions that arise from pure consciousness, that are independent of prior mental conditioning, are pure actions; they are not reactions.

In our daily living, we may perhaps feel we are performing actions, but in reality most of us are generally not acting, but rather reacting. Ask yourself, "Am I performing an action, or merely reacting to the other person or situation?" Whenever you feel the need to act impulsively, take a pause and dip into the stillness beyond thoughts. In doing so, you are consulting the Source within you. This practice will enable you to raise your awareness and take inspired actions. You can then lead an awakened life of joy and creativity.

With raised awareness, you become conscious of the space where you can choose your response. Further, when awareness is absorbed in itself, it is called Self-awareness. Consciousness becomes conscious of itself in and through every activity. When every activity makes you aware of your essential presence, to the awareness of the Self, you begin to abide in pure consciousness. In this sublime state, you are only present. All actions happen merely in your presence. You shift from 'doing' to spontaneous 'happening'. When action is performed from this space, the action is not a reaction. All work performed this way is Bright Action, which liberates you.

23. What is karmic bondage? What is the cause of bondage to karma?

Sirshree: Karmic bondage is the result of the belief that you are a separate individual. The feeling of separateness from totality is the original sin. We always contemplate on the second sin, the secondary ego. The secondary ego is merely symptoms like exaggerated self-pride and arrogance. The primary ego is the belief that you are separate from everyone else.

Most spiritual practices deal with methods of eliminating the secondary ego - the defilements like anger, hatred, fear, anxiety etc. But, this cannot lead to liberation, as the primary ego has not been dealt with. If we eliminate the primary ego (the original sin), then the secondary ego will not exist; the secondary sin won't occur. We forget our true identity and live the life of separate limited individuals in ignorance. Actions that arise based on the assumed individual identity is sin; actions that arise based on the understanding of who-we-truly-are is the greatest virtue.

Most often, actions are performed with a feeling of doer-ship ("I did it"). We think, "I made this happen." Or "Oh! I shouldn't have done this; it's wrong." With such feelings, the individual egoic 'I' is strengthened and we become bound to karma.

By repeating the same behaviour or thought again and again, a pattern or tendency is formed. As we repeat our preconditioned behaviour, our tendencies become deep-rooted. The habit of doing any deed in the same way again and again is tendency. We are not alert before or while acting. From morning till night, most of the deeds that happen could be the unconscious enactment of tendencies. This predisposition of helplessly acting by our tendencies is yet another cause for bondage to karma.

Pure consciousness, pure love, is rooted in oneness. It knows no distinction or duality. Life naturally brings us the experience of love, bliss, peace, health, harmony, vitality and abundance. There is nothing in this world that can negatively impact us, except our own beliefs, our own thoughts and emotions. However, when we assume the limited body-mind as 'I', then it gives birth to the illusory notion of 'others'. This naturally gives rise to delusion, resulting in emotions like anger, fear, greed, hatred, envy, ill-will and resentment.

When we entertain such negative emotions in ignorance of our true nature, we succumb to the illusion of separateness. In doing so, we actually resist the flow of life through our bodies. Negative, hurtful memories, bitterness, and ill-will choke the free flow of life within us. When one holds onto grudges in life, one feels bitterness and resentment. This clogs the free flow of vital energy. If we feel bitter and hold grudges, in time, it eventually affects our physical wellbeing, causing chronic ailments.

By feeling resentment towards any person or situation, we actually plant seeds of hatred. We unknowingly place an order for even more resentment that rebounds back on us, multiplied many times over. We do this unknowingly due to lack of awareness. With every act in our past where we have either felt hurt or caused others to feel hurt, we create a string of bondage that blocks free flow in our lives. Holding onto negative emotions causes blocks in energy pathways within the mind-body mechanism. These blocks manifest as physiological malfunctions, leading to disease conditions, which eventually erupt as visible symptoms. Chronic headaches, ulcers, indigestion, kidney failures, cancer, are all caused by sustained intensification of negative emotions over long periods of time.

When you resist the free flow of life, you experience testing circumstances, limitations and sorrow. Thoughts, feelings, words and actions that have arisen from the ignorant belief of separateness bind you and choke the expression of life. This is the manifest form of karmic bondage. Actually, these limitations and sorrow come as wake-up calls to re-connect and re-align with the natural flow of the Self. They come as reminders to recognize and honour the essential Oneness of everything. This has been explained in short, but this subject is deep and subtle, and has vast implications.

We need to get rid of these karmic bonds by performing Bright actions that assert the truth of who-we-truly-are. This will open the doors to liberation from karmic bondage. You will then effectively continue to perform the highest actions without incurring any karmic bondage.

24. I am beginning to understand what karmic bondage truly is. How can we attain liberation from karmic bondage?

Sirshree: Actions are not merely physical actions. Actions happen first at the mental level and could then manifest as speech and physical action. This is a missing link in understanding the Law of Karma. People believe that they are performing the right deeds when their externally visible speech and actions are positive and virtuous. However, the feelings and the self-talk that goes on within the mind is also action. Karmic cleansing needs to happen at the mental level. The external manifestation will then be automatically dealt with.

Actions that bind you happen out of ignorance of who-you-truly-are due to enactment of tendencies. Bright actions arise from the understanding of your true nature. The thought of the individual 'I' needs to be uprooted with the fire of understanding. When we attain understanding, then none of the karma performed through our body will cause bondage.

When a man uses a chisel and hammer to carve a line on stone, this line remains for a long period. Similarly, some deeds have a deep impact on life. We suffer the pain of remorse and hatred for a long period during our lives due to such deeds. Some deeds are like lines drawn on sand. The effects last for a short time. After a while the effects vanish. There are some deeds that are like lines drawn on water. When lines are drawn in water, they vanish as soon as they are made. These deeds bear fruit immediately.

Finally, there are some deeds that are like lines drawn in the sky. Such lines can never be formed. Bright deeds are like these lines. They don't result in bondage. Bright fresh actions originate from the realization of the Self, from the standpoint of Oneness. The impressions of prior tendencies no longer function. You remain in the present and all your responses arise from the recognition of your true nature as pure consciousness. When consciousness is absorbed in itself, actions do not bind. You are only present as a pure Self-witness. All actions happen merely in your presence.

But how do we get rid of past karmic bondage? How do we free ourselves from the umpteen problems and difficulties of life and move towards total liberation? The answer: through the practice of forgiveness!

Forgiveness is not merely about seeking or accepting apologies; it has a deeper aspect to it. Forgiveness is a matter of the heart; not words. Forgiveness involves sensitivity, awareness, compassion and love. Forgiveness completely wipes away hatred, resentment and ego. It increases the purity and piousness of the mind. Forgiveness is a conscious, deliberate decision to release feelings of resentment or vengeance towards anyone, even yourself. You surrender everything that has happened to the Self instead of blaming yourself or others.

Forgiveness brings you peace of mind and frees you from corrosive anger. Forgiveness does not mean condoning or excusing a serious offence that someone may have committed against you. You need not reconcile with the person who seriously harmed you if you don't want to. It involves letting go of deeply held negative feelings. In this way, it empowers you to recognize the pain you suffered without letting that pain define you, enabling you to heal and move on with your life.

The essence of forgiveness encompasses a much deeper and wider dimension. Forgiveness is actually an all-curing panacea for all the negativity and problems that fill your life and that of the whole world. It clears karmic bondages and fills us with divine love, joy and peace.

Forgiveness is all about erasing karmic bondages that tie us down in the rigours of worldly life and relations, preventing us from moving towards liberation. Every time you entertain impure and negative feelings for someone, a karmic line gets drawn on the whiteboard of pure consciousness, linking the two of you in a karmic bondage. Pure consciousness does not remain pure. It gets tainted with these impressions. Since most people in the world are unaware of this law, they keep piling several such lines of bondage. As a result the universal consciousness that permeates the world becomes polluted, thereby obscuring its purity.

The complete practice of forgiveness consists of four aspects:

- Seeking forgiveness from people for negative feelings that you have harboured for them and any hurtful feelings that you may have caused them
- Forgiving people for hurtful feelings that they may have caused you

- Seeking forgiveness from yourself, your mind-body mechanism for knowingly or unknowingly favouring negativity, ignorance, and tormenting your own mind and body
- Seeking forgiveness from the Source (God) collectively for yourself and on behalf of others.

If you practice this consistently with conviction, not a single line of karmic bondage will remain on your whiteboard of pure consciousness. You will start experiencing divine love, joy and peace.

The best way to remain free from karmic bondage is to not create them. For this you will have to raise your awareness to such a level that as soon as you get the slightest hint of negativity arising in your mind towards somebody, you will instantly erase it. But until you get to this level of awareness, you can start by erasing karmic bondage at least once a day. All such lines of bondage that are already present on your whiteboard of consciousness need to be erased. Even if a single line remains on it, your liberation is at stake.

While you cleanse karmic bondage of the past, you can raise your awareness to ensure that you do not draw any further karmic lines in the present. The practice of true meditation helps you raise your awareness, so that your actions are imbued with understanding.

25. What is true meditation? What are the missing links in the practice of meditation?

Sirshree: First, understand what is NOT meditation. Meditation is not attention. It is not concentration or contemplation. Today, the meaning of meditation has been misconstrued. The words attention, contemplation, and meditation are used interchangeably and the word has lost its deeper significance.

When you say, "I am meditating on the next course of action," you are actually contemplating. You are in thoughts, dealing with the content of thoughts. When you say, "I am meditating on the candle-flame," this is merely concentration. It is about focusing your attention on a single object of attention. Most people practice techniques pertaining to the body and mind, only to attain a high degree of concentration. However, this is far from the essence of meditation.

There are many who practice what is known as 'mindfulness'. Mindfulness is the practice of being aware of what's happening in the present at the levels of the mind and body. They observe every action, every movement and consider that as meditation. Again, mindfulness has its benefits in terms of calming the mind. However, mindfulness is not meditation.

Now understand what IS meditation. Meditation is the nature of the Self; it is your essential nature. You ARE meditation! Meditation is the state of the Self when it is absorbed in itself.

If you want to understand meditation in terms of a practice, then the simple meaning of meditation is 'doing nothing.' However, some people find 'doing nothing' very difficult. They try to do 'nothing' instead of 'doing nothing.' Mediation is beyond 'doing' and 'non-doing', because it exists in 'being'. People question how it's possible to do 'nothing'. It's like asking, "What should I do to fall asleep?" You have to do nothing to fall asleep. You just need to lie down. If you try, sleep won't happen. It's an effortless process. Similarly, meditation is a process in which you don't need to do anything; your very presence, in essence, is meditation. You just allow meditation to happen.

When we're caught up in things of the external world like relationships, wealth, status, or power, all our senses get completely engrossed in them. Meditation, when viewed as a path, is a technique that liberates us from the attachments and aversions of the external world and directs us within, onto the experience of pure conscious presence. All our senses, which are focused on the external world, should be redirected within. This is the initial preparation for entering into meditation.

It is important to understand that liberation from the external world is not the real purpose. This is only the preparation for the real purpose.

Due to this missing link, meditation has been misunderstood and limited to the practice of moving your focus away from the world. The original purpose of meditation techniques is to stabilize in the conscious presence of the Self, followed by expression that arises from that state. In order to refer to this original purpose without causing confusion, we may use a new term: Self-meditation.

Self-meditation is being one with the Source of everything; being established in the seat of pure consciousness. In this state, the knower becomes aware of the knower through everything that is being known. Self-meditation is the path and also the ultimate goal. It is like a double-headed arrow; when attention is directed to the world, it is also being directed to the source of attention. The experiencer experiences the experiencer through every experience. Every experience serves as a mirror to experience the knower.

During meditation, all kinds of thoughts arise. These thoughts torment us because we're attached and identified with them. You are the witness of these thoughts. You are not the thoughts. All the thoughts that are buried deep within you have to emerge and be encountered by the witness. The mind is annihilated in this process. When you move beyond the content of your thoughts and learn to use thoughts merely as a pretext to return your attention on the knowing awareness, this is Self-mediation. This is the missing link and also the purpose of meditation.

❖ ❖ ❖

You can mail your opinion or feedback on this book to: books.feedback@tejgyan.org

About Sirshree

Sirshree's spiritual quest, which began during his childhood, led him on a journey through various schools of philosophy and meditation practices. He studied a wide range of literature on mind science and spirituality. After a long period of deep contemplation on the truth of life, his quest culminated in attaining the ultimate truth.

Sirshree espouses, "All spiritual paths that lead to the truth begin differently but culminate at the same point – Understanding. This understanding is complete in itself. Listening to this understanding is enough to attain the Truth." Over the last two decades, he has dedicated his life to raise mass consciousness.

Sirshree has delivered more than 4000 discourses that throw light on this understanding. He has designed a system for wisdom, which makes it accessible to all. This system has inspired people from all walks of life to progress on their journey of the Truth. Thousands of seekers join in a virtual prayer for World Peace and Global Healing daily at 9:09 am and 9:09 pm.

About Tej Gyan Foundation

Tej Gyan Foundation is a non-profit organization founded on the teachings of Sirshree. The Foundation disseminates Tejgyan – the wisdom that guides one from self-development to Self-realization, leading towards Self-stabilization.

The Foundation's system for imparting wisdom has been assessed by international quality auditors and accredited with the ISO 9001:2015 certification. This wisdom has been presented in a simple, systematic, and practically applicable form that makes it accessible to people from all walks of life, regardless of religion, caste, social strata, country, or belief system.

The Foundation has centers in more than 400 cities and towns across India and other countries. The mission of Tej Gyan Foundation is to create a highly evolved society by leading seekers from negative thoughts to positive thoughts and further, from positive thoughts to Happy thoughts. A 'Happy thought' is the auspicious thought of being free from all thoughts, leading to the state of supreme bliss beyond thoughts.

If you seek such wisdom that leads you beyond mere knowledge, dissolves all problems, frees you from all limiting beliefs, reveals the true nature of divinity, and establishes you in the ultimate truth, then it is time to discover Tejgyan; it is time to rise above the mundane knowledge of words and experience Tejgyan!

The MahaAasmani Magic of Awakening Retreat

Self-development to Self-realization towards Self-stabilization

Do you wish to experience unconditional happiness that is not dependent on any reason? Happiness that is permanent and only increases with time? Do you wish to experience love, peace, self-belief, harmony in relationships, prosperity, and true contentment? Do you wish to progress in all facets of your life, viz. physical, mental, social, financial, and spiritual?

If you seek answers to these questions and are thirsty for the ultimate truth, then you are welcome to participate in the MahaAasmani Magic of Awakening retreat organized by Tej Gyan Foundation. This is the Foundation's flagship retreat based on the teachings of Sirshree.

The purpose of this retreat

The purpose of this retreat is that every human being should:

- Discover the answer to "Who am I" and "Why am I?" through direct experience and be established in ultimate bliss.

- Learn the art of living in the present, free from the burden of the past and the anxiety of the future.

- Acquire practical tools to help quieten the chattering mind and dissolve problems.

- Discover missing links in the practices of Meditation (*Dhyana*), Action (*Karma*), Wisdom (*Gyana*), and Devotion (*Bhakti*).

About Books by Sirshree

Sirshree's published work includes more than 150 book titles, some of which have been translated into more than 10 languages. His literature provides a profound reading on various topics of practical living and unravels the missing links in karma, wisdom, devotion, meditation, and consciousness.

His books have been published by leading publishing houses like Penguin, Hay House, Bloomsbury, Wisdom Tree, Jaico, etc. "The Source" book series, authored by Sirshree, has sold over 10 million copies. Various luminaries and celebrities like His Holiness the Dalai Lama, publishers Mr. Reid Tracy, Ms. Tami Simon and Yoga Master Dr. B. K. S. Iyengar have released Sirshree's books and lauded his work.

The Source
Attain Both, Inner Peace
and Worldly success

Awaken the Power of Faith
Discover the 7 Principles of the
Highest Power of the Universe

To order books authored by Sirshree, login to:
www.gethappythoughts.org
For further details, call: +91 9011013210

SELECT BOOKS AUTHORED BY SIRSHREE

   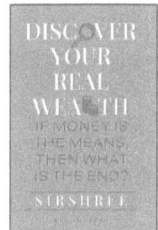

To order these and other books authored by Sirshree
Visit **www.gethappythoughts.org**

Tej Gyan Foundation – Contact details

Registered Office:
Happy Thoughts Building, Vikrant Complex, Near Tapovan Mandir, Pimpri, Pune 411017, INDIA. Contact: +91 20-27411240, +91 20-27412576

MaNaN Ashram:
Survey No. 43, Sanas Nagar, Nandoshi Gaon, Kirkatwadi Phata, Off Sinhagad Road, Taluka Haveli, Pune district - 411024, INDIA. Contact: +91 992100 8060.

WORLD PEACE PRAYER

Divine Light of Love, Bliss, and Peace is Showering;
The Golden Light of Higher Consciousness is Rising;
All negativity on Earth is Dissolving;
Everyone is in Peace and Blissfully Shining;
O God, Gratitude for Everything!

Members of Tej Gyan Foundation have been offering this impersonal mass prayer for many years. Those who are happy can offer this prayer. Those feeling low or suffering from illness can receive healing with this prayer.

If you are feeling troubled or sick, please sit to receive the healing effect of this prayer. Visualize that the divine white healing light is being showered on earth through the prayers of thousands and is also reaching you, bringing you peace and good health. You can dwell in this feeling for some time and then offer your gratitude to those offering the prayer.

A Humble Appeal

More than a million peace lovers pray for World Peace and Global Healing every morning and evening at 9:09. Also, a prayer (in Hindi) to elevate consciousness is webcast every day on YouTube at 3:30 pm and 9:00 pm IST. Please participate in this noble endeavor.